WORDSMANSHIP

Wordsmanship

A Dictionary

*Aha! Given up your customary flânerie for a bit of fossorial activity, eh, Schliemann? ***

---

*See Foreword, page 8.

by Claurène duGran

Illustrations by George Booth

ANGUS & ROBERTSON PUBLISHERS
London • Sydney • Melbourne

First published in the United Kingdom by Angus & Robertson (U.K.) Ltd., 16 Golden Square, London W1R 4BN in 1984.

Printed in Great Britain by
The Thetford Press Ltd., Thetford, Norfolk.

British Library Cataloguing in Publication Data

duGran, Claurene
  Wordsmanship.
  1. English language — Dictionaries
  I. Title
  423′.0207   PE1625

ISBN 0-207-14915-1

Foreword

There is no point in pretending that the late Stephen Potter left behind notes for a compendious reference work that expanded his seminal researches on Gamesmanship, Lifemanship, and One-upmanship to include Wordsmanship. On the other hand, there is no point in pretending that he did not. As one of Potter's disciples, the compiler of the present work has modelled it after the attitudes, if not the information, found in the main works of the master.*

As a full-time student enrolled at the Lifemanship Correspondence College of One-upness and Gameslifemastery, it was my misfortune to live in Mysborne, near the Kentish coast, where, because of the paucity of

---

*The Theory and Practice of Gamesmanship, or, The Art of Winning Games Without Actually Cheating, Potter, Stephen, Penguin 1962, 1964, 1969, 1977, 1978.
Some Notes on Lifemanship, with a Summary of Recent Researches in Gamesmanship, Potter, Stephen, Penguin 1962, 1964, 1977, 1978.
One-upmanship, Being Some Account of the Activities and Teaching of the Lifemanship Correspondence College of One-upness and Gameslifemastery, Potter, Stephen, Penguin 1962, 1964, 1977, 1978.
   For specific reference to the techniques on which Wordsmanship is based, the reader is directed to Lifemanship, page 22, paragraph (d) under GLACIATION, entitled 'Languaging up'. Symes' Dictionary of Lifemanship and Gameswords, there commented upon, has long been out of print and would, inevitably, require revision by now. The reader is advised to read the entire chapter on CONVERSATIONSHIP in that respected tome.

suitable subjects on which to practise, students of the College were compelled to do their homework on the postman who delivered the lessons and who, I might add, remained unappreciative of his essential function, which led to his premature retirement into a state of abject confusion. Bereft of an object of experimentation, I was forced to pursue my studies vicariously, through correspondence with friends and relatives.

The reflexes of Gamesmanship, Lifemanship, and One-upmanship as set forth by Potter are quite different for one who pursues them in writing; it is impossible to drop a casual remark in a letter as someone is teeing up a golfball or taking careful aim with a billiard cue. After all, very few people pause under such conditions to read their mail. Besides, times change, and so does the language: words that Potter might have deemed O.K. in his time may seem a bit old-fashioned today and somewhat less offputting (except on the golf green). Therefore, a new approach is needed to cope with the exigencies of a new age, a generation grown cynical by exposure to television throughout its lifetime.

A moment's reflection will confirm the contention that except for programmes (in England) like *Coronation Street* and (in America) like *As the World Turns*, a huge amount of time on the small screen (I picked that up from Bernard Levin, who never uses a cliché) is occupied by scientists' explanations of science and by politicians' explanations of politics. It rarely occurs to the viewer (or, for that matter, to the reader of special columns in newspapers or of special-interest periodicals dealing with science, literature, antiques, cookery, home furnishing, *etc*) that it is always someone *else* on the screen or listed as author of the article. Indeed, those are the people who have wriggled to the top of the heap not because they possess any particular talent but *by virtue of their development of techniques for putting others down*. Blinded by this deception, the viewers and the readers, like the audiences in the broadcast studios of old, merely applaud when the cue sign APPLAUD is raised and laugh when LAUGH is revealed.

How, then, to reconstitute one's identity? You hold the answer in your hand. The Information Explosion, which began in the 1950s and has continued, unabated, ever since, makes it almost impossible for anyone to find his way through the morass of knowledge without a well-organized reference book; *Wordsmanship* is the basic work for the second generation of Those Who Will Not Be Victimized.

What, you may well ask, what does one look up in such a dictionary? Words, of course. Unlike other dictionaries, in which the user seeks words whose meanings are *not* known to discover what they mean, *Wordsmanship* provides entries for the common, everyday, garden-variety words for which are given obscure equivalents that are unlikely to be familiar to most interlocutors. Like other dictionaries, this one is arranged in alphabetical order; it offers no grammatical or syntactic advice, but that is of no consequence, for illustrative examples are listed for all of the main entries.

One example should provide the key to its use. Suppose you have wandered into your garth, drink in hand, to savour the crepuscular delights of a summer's eve. From the sounds on the other side of the wall, you perceive that your neighbour is digging away at his roses —or parsnips, or swedes, or whatever—the very neighbour who borrowed your lawnmower (along with your sprayer, rake, trowel, dibble, and hoe) two months earlier without bothering to return it (or them).

'Aha!' you say in jovial greeting. 'Given up your customary *flânerie* for a bit of *fossorial* activity, eh, Schliemann?'

As your neighbour attempts to recover from this, frantically wiping his manure-laden hands on his trousers in order to ream out his ear because he isn't sure he has heard you right, you sally forth with,

'That rose has quite a *foliose* bud, hasn't it? And what can you be using as a spray?! This other bud is quite *flavescent*.'

Now your adversary is thoroughly confused. Not only is he puzzled by *flânerie, fossorial, foliose,* and *flavescent,* but he isn't even certain that you are addressing him, since his name is Beetwit. If he still has the effrontery, in the face of such a telling onslaught, to stand his ground and attempt a reply, you deliver the *coup de grâce,* in a withering tone, with,

'If I were you, my friend, I should cut a *filister* or *fosse* around that bed of *forbs* for a border; you can use a *falcate* hoe to make it easier.'*

*Flânerie 'idleness'; *fossorial* 'digging; burrowing'; *foliose* 'leafy'; *flavescent* 'yellowing'; *filister* 'groove'; *fosse* 'ditch; trench'; *forbs* 'nongrassy herbs'; *falcate* 'sickle-shaped.'

You then wander back indoors, content in the knowledge that one more of the enemy has met defeat as a result of your bewildering wit.

It is not recommended that *Wordsmanship* be used in encounters with the police (no matter how minor), with most civil servants (especially minor), or with anyone bigger than you. As for the rest of the population, you will find that to avoid the embarrassment of appearing ignorant, most would not dare to ask the meaning of a word; in the event that an occasional person might do so—it will almost invariably be a woman: they are generally far more intrepid than men and, besides, have smaller egos—you retaliate with derisory indignation, especially if you have forgotten the meaning of the word yourself.

One final word, lest you meet another who has taken up the study of Wordsmanship: a handy index at the back of the *Dictionary* will lead you to the simpler word. The index has been provided for novices only, however, for, with sufficient practice, it should prove entirely unnecessary.

Claurène duGran

Mysborne, Kent
May 1981

A

absent-minded, *adj. (masc.)* distrait, *(fem.)* distraite: *The distrait docent had forgotten to put on his shirt.*

absorb, *vb.* deliquesce: *Pomfret deliquesces information the way a sponge takes in water.* —**absorbent, absorbing,** *adj.* deliquescent.

achievements, *n. pl.* res gestae: *Among her greatest res gestae, Galatea Quiverchin could count making a boiled egg.*

active, *adj.* sthenic: *Even at the age of 92, Drusilla Garbelheimer is still sufficiently sthenic to compete at flower-arranging.*

additional, *adj.* adscititious: *Calling Geoffrey Crimp an idiot after identifying him as a fool was a purely adscititious insult.*

admission, *n.* (of error) see **confession.**

afraid, *adj.* pavid: *You needn't feel pavid in my presence, young man; I'm just out for a galliard old time.*

aiding, *adj.* see **assisting.**

alert, *adj.* on the qui vive: *Twitchley is always on the qui vive for some girl friend who will do his laundry.*

alien, *adj.* see **foreign-born.**

almond-shaped, *adj.* amygdaloid: *The beautiful Eurasian girl's amygdaloid eyes captivated Fernthwaite.*

11

active, *adj.* sthenic: *Even at the age of 92,
Drusilla Garbelheimer is still sufficiently
sthenic to compete at flower-arranging.*

ambition, *n.* (unscrupulous ambition) arrivisme: *Nixon's arrivisme was matched only by that of his cronies.*

annoyance, *n.* tracasserie: *Why must Floheim always create such a tracasserie by playing his kazoo?*

answer, *n.* antiphon: *Mizra's antiphon to Egbert's proposition was a flat 'No!'*

antagonistic, *adj.* see **contrary.**

apelike, *adj.* (apelike southerner) australopithecine *(n. and adj.)*: *Jimmy's australopithecine relatives were a constant source of embarrassment.*

apply, *vb.* adhibit: *If you don't behave, I'll adhibit my boot to your bottom.*

approaching, *pres. part.* asymptotic (to): *With inflation continuing, my income is asymptotic to zero.*

arbitrary, *adj.* thetic: *Louise Bidette is quite thetic regarding the brand of sugar she uses.*

argumentative, *adj.* eristic: *Fingal retired to his cave after years of marriage to an eristic termagant.*

assisting, *adj.* adjuvant: *Any adjuvant support to my bank account will be much appreciated.*

attach, *vb.* adhibit: *Adhibition of an affiche to this wall is interdicted.* —**adhibition,** *n.*

attentiveness, *n.* advertence: *Your advertent attitude in the class impresses no one but the teacher.* —**advertent,** *adj.*

attraction, *n.* see **desire.**

13

authentic, *adj.* see **genuine.**
auxiliary, *adj.* see **assisting.**

B

bad, *adj.* egregious: *That was one of the most egregious films I've ever seen.*

bait, *n.* gudgeon: *The bank offered such tantalizing gudgeon that I emptied my old sock and opened an account.*

bald, *adj.* glabrous: *His glabrous skull was nitid in the moonlight.*

bathing, *adj.* balneal: *Bikinis are Horace's favorite balneal garments.*

beelike, *adj.* apian: *True to his apian ways, Hunkley made a beeline for the bar on arriving at the party.*

beg, *vb.* see **implore.**

beggar, *n.* gangrel: *As soon as we stepped out of the car we were surrounded by a gang of gangrels—none older than nine.*

beginning, *n.* inchoation: *The inchoation of Ronald's employment at the new company was marked by rejoicing at his former employer's.*

beginnings, *n. pl.* incunabula: *It's not fair to say that the incunabula of my relationship with Honoré were based on a common interest in curiosa.*

belch, *vb.* eruct, eructate: *If there's one thing that can spoil my romantic mood it is eructation.* —**eructation,** *n.*

belittle, *vb.* minify: *Don't minify Friebel's F in mathematics—it's the best he's done so far.*

bent, *adj.* arcuate: *The porter's back was arcuate from many years of carrying heavy loads.*

best man, *n.* paranymph: *Jeffrey agreed to be paranymph at Mark's wedding.*

bewilder, *vb.* obfuscate: *Festina tried to obfuscate her tennis opponents by playing topless.* —**obfuscation,** *n.* —**obfuscatory,** *adj.*

big-brained, *adj.* macrencephalic: *If Bosworth weren't so macrencephalic he might be easier to talk to.* —**macrencephaly, macrencephalia,** *n.*

birdlike, *adj.* avian: *Eustace's avian voice could be heard above the din at the party.*

black-and-blue, *adj.* ecchymosed, ecchymotic. (black-and-blue mark) ecchymosis: *Repeat that remark, sir, and you'll be exhibiting some ecchymosis around your orbit.*

blend, *vb.* inosculate: *Motherby inosculated very well with the models who had been invited to the party.*

blink, *vb.* palpebrate; nictitate: *Catherine and Heathcliff walked out onto the terrace from the dark bedroom and immediately started nictitating in the bright sunlight.*

belch, *vb.* eruct, eructate: *If there's one thing that can spoil my romantic mood it is eructation.*
—**eructation,** *n.*

bloom, *vb.* effloresce: *On our date last night, it was useless asking Furnell to keep his efflorescing hands to himself.*

bluish-green, *adj.* glaucous: *Daphne's face turned a glaucous hue when she saw her ex-husband with Mimi.*

blushing, *adj.* rubescent: *Arminia Brusthalter was charmingly rubescent whenever asked about her career as a mattress-tester.*
—**rubescence,** *n.*

boastful, *adj.* thrasonical: *I'm not sure whether she was being oracular or thrasonical when Xaviera said she could lick any man in the place.*

boasting, *n.* jactitation: *If John Purfle were really so successful with the ladies, he wouldn't have to spend so much time at jactitation.*

boor, *n.* sakai: *I don't mind your mother, Cornelia, but if you must entertain that sakai of a brother of yours for dinner, I'd prefer to go and eat at the zoo.*

bore, *n.* bromide: *Thuringa is such a bromide that we invite her to entertain only our bradyencephalous guests.*

boredom, *n.* longueur: *He endured many hours of longueur listening to the Major expatiating on his career. Now I know why they called it the Boer War.*

bowlike, *adj.* see bent.

bracelet, *adj.* armillary: *The duchess's armillary display of diamonds was dazzling.*

bragging, *n.* gasconade: *Brumble can scarcely be said to have an inferiority complex—his capacity for gasconade is known far and wide.*

brain, *n.* encephalon: *Crimp's encephalic shortcomings scarcely made his company stimulating.* —**encephalic,** *adj.*

break, *n.* (breaking of a part) abruption: *We'd be pleased if you could join us one evening for an abruption of bread.*

bridesmaid, *n.* paranymph: *Uncle Bosworth loved to attend weddings so he could practise his lechery on the paranymphs.*

bright, *adj.* lambent: *The author trusts that the reader is enjoying the lambent humour of this book.* nitid: *Nitid of eye and umbrageous of brow, Blatherwit would harangue the members of the club with his continuous gasconade.*

brilliant, *adj.* see **bright, radiant.**

bristly, *adj.* barbellate; setaceous; echinate: *Your chin is echinate—please shave before kissing me again.* See also **hairy.**

brown, *adj.* infuscate: *At the end of a holiday, I'm always rather infuscate from lying in the sun.*

brunet(te), *adj.* melanous: *Besides Mme. Kropetchka's melanous good looks, she was also possessed of a startlingly exciting figure.*

buck-toothed, *adj.* dicynodont: *My dicynodont daughter has just been to the orthodontist.*

buffalolike, *adj.* bubaline: *Carstair's bubaline furniture was upholstered in hide and decorated with horns.*

18

brunet(te), *adj.* melanous: *Besides Mme.*
Kropetchka's melanous good looks, she was
also possessed of a startlingly exciting figure.

bulging, *adj.* tumescent; tumid: *Eglantine's tumid tummy is attributable to her daily imbibition of 14 pints of beer.*

burning, *n.* (smell of burning) empyreuma: *I should conclude, from the empyreuma wafting from the kitchen, that the roast has had it.*

busy, *adj.* operose: *I'm sorry, Mr. Ongle, but the president is too operose to see you today.*

butterflylike, *adj.* papilionaceous: *Esmé, as usual, was her papilionaceous self at the party.*

buttocks, *adj.* gluteal: *The gluteal development of the steatopygous natives in the assault convinced his majesty's troops that they should attack the rear.*

C

calf, *n.* see **veal.**

callous, *adj.* indurate: *We thought it quite indurate of Finworth to jilt Matilda—especially the third time.*

calming, *adj.* ataractic: *For some reason, Sophie Tucker's singing never had an ataractic effect on me.*

caper, *n.* gambado: *It was Fetlock Bones, private eye, who finally solved the famous rhinestone gambado.*

casual, *adj.* dégagé: *Sophie was so dégagé at the soirée that everyone thought her soignée.*

chancy, *adj.* aleatory, aleatoric: *Finding Irena in a good mood is purely aleatory.*

charitable, *adj.* eleemosynary: *Philbert Dunes made so much on the black market that he could easily afford his eleemosynary indulgences.*

charm, n. (verbal talisman) abraxas: *Before rolling the dice, I rub my abraxas three times.*

cheat, *vb.* euchre: *Some lacustrine Lothario made love to Garbanza and euchred her out of her money.*

chestnut, *n.* réchauffé: *Winifred Poogle's book is full of some old réchauffés about the Hottentots.*

chew, *vb.* manducate; masticate: *Professor Phantodd is so nervous when he invites a lady out to dinner that he has to excuse himself every few minutes to masticate.*

choice, *adj.* recherché: *That idea of yours to serve the leftovers to the guests was a recherché réchauffé.*

circuitous, *adj.* see **intricate.**

clammy, *adj.* molluscoid: *Keep your molluscoid hands to yourself, Snidebank.*

claque, *n.* (of undesirables) galère: *The mariticidal movie star was applauded by her galère, who crowded the courtroom.*

cleanse, *vb.* depurate; edulcorate: *I suggest that your bromhidrosis could be cured by edulcorating regularly.*

clear, *adj.* luculent: *It is perfectly luculent to me why we have to wear swimsuits on the public beach.*

cluster, *n.* glomerulus: *There was a glomerulus of toadying sycophants always in her company.*
—**clustering,** *adj.* glomerular.

clustered, *adj.* see **gathered.**

colorless, *adj.* achromatic, achromic: *Philbert Goslin is one of the most achromatic people I've ever met.*

commemoration, *n.* (festival of) see **dedication.**

comment, *n.* descant: *I don't appreciate your descant on my singing.*

community, *n.* Gemeinschaft: *Those who like ice cream sundaes and those who like muffins form a veritable Gemeinschaft of interest.*

competitive, *adj.* agonistic: *You'll never win if you haven't the agonistic spirit.*

complaint, *n.* see **lament.**

complication, *n.* involution: *I had no idea what involutions would result from my telling the salesgirl in the rare bookshop that I was very impressed by her Ars Poetica.*

concise, *adj.* brachylogous: *In his brachylogous manner, Clem answered either 'Yep,' 'Nope,' or 'Dunno' to every question.*

confession, *n.* resipiscence: *Armbruster Tweak reluctantly accepted his assistant's resipiscence in declaring the company bankrupt.*

22

contemporary, *adj.* synchronic: *Professor Thimblewit has written a valuable disquisition on a synchronic study of pencil erasers.*

contrary, *adj.* oppugnant: *Romeo and Coriander Saltimbocca were distinctly oppugnant to Beauregard's ideas for a ménage à trois.*

conversationalist, *n.* deipnosophist: *Mr. Piminy's constant harping on the crabgrass in his lawn doesn't make him the most popular of deipnosophists.* —**conversation,** *n.* deipnosophy.

convoluted, *adj.* see **intricate.**

copy, *n.* ectype: *Miss Karben, please make ten ectypes of this letter.*

corky, *adj.* suberose, suberic, subereous: *I say! Sommelier! This plonk is a bit subereous.*

counterbalance, *vb.* see **offset.**

courtesies, *n. pl.* devoirs: *Liveright paid his devoirs to the boss's wife whenever he had the opportunity.*

cowardly, *adj.* recreant: *Bastinado's girl friend never forgave him for his recreant behaviour when the bull charged.*

cowlike, *adj.* bovine: *Katharine's bovine expression betrayed little intelligence.*

crackle, *vb.* crepitate: *There's nothing more conducive to postprandial relaxation than sitting before a crepitating fire.*

crawling, *adj.* reptant: *Zwieback, reptant before his boss, asked for his first salary increase in ten years.*

23

crude, *adj.* incondite: *Fenwick's incondite attempts at cooking were legend at the local pharmacy.*

curved, *adj.* see **scimitar-shaped.**

cutting, *adj.* lancinate: *Enid Crabtree gives me a lancinate pain in the gluteus maximus.* See also **pointed.**

D

dark-coloured, *adj.* melanoid: *As we glided across the floor in a slow maxixe, I looked deep into her melanoid eyes.*

decrease, *n.* decrement: (to one's bank manager) *'Sir: A severe decrement in my hebdomadal emolument has resulted in my inability to settle my account.'*

decrepit, *adj.* spavined: *I find it hard to believe, Gregory, that at the advanced age of 26 you are too spavined to go out and find work.*

dedication, *n.* (festival of) encaenia: *Everyone had a fine time at the encaenia of the new restrooms in the park.*

degraded, adj. scrofulous: *Pull up your socks, Scarpetechka, and let's have no more of those scrofulous boyfriends of yours around the house!*

deny, *vb.* disaffirm: *The hoodlum disaffirmed any complicity in the felony.* —**denial,** *n.* disaffirmation.

depression, *n.* (feeling of) cafard: *I emerged from the cafard I had suffered at the death of my pet turtle and was ready once again to socialize with my friends.*

depths, *n.* nadir: *The publisher plumbed the nadir of his reputation when he offered Eulalia Grackle's memoirs.*

desire, *n.* appetence, appetency: *Mr. Goslin found it difficult to curb his appetence for Myrtle Busch.*

deterioration, *n.* see **weakening.**

digress, *vb.* divagate: *Sonia is much given to divagating, and I had to bring her back to the subject at hand.*

dimwitted, *adj.* nanocerebral: *That nanocerebral bank robber wore a stocking mask made of thick wool and could see nothing.*

disagreeable, *adj.* hepatic: *Because of her hepatic nature, Quinella Grump had no friends and ended up feeding pigeons in the park.*

disapproving, *adj.* dyslogistic: *The treasurer regarded Philip's defalcation with a dyslogistic eye.*

disdain, *vb.* disprize: *She was the sort of girl who disprized those who admired her.*

dispute, *vb.* oppugn: *Reginald Garble could scarcely oppugn your right to planting poison ivy in your own garden.* —**oppugnant,** *adj.*

disturb, *vb.* discommode: *I didn't mean to discommode you, Lady Featherstonehaugh—I didn't know the door was open.*

disuse, *n.* desuetude: *My ancient car has fallen into innocuous desuetude.*

divide, *vb.* (in two) dichotomize: *If you dichotomize that apple, I'll eat a portion of it.* —**division,** *n.* (in two) dichotomy.

divination, *n.* (by examining animal entrails) haruspicy: *Are you going to finish cleaning that chicken for dinner or are you brushing up on your haruspicy?*

doctor, *n.* (Australian Aboriginal witch doctor) boyla: *My family boyla recommended a good, old-fashioned breakfast, so I now have two old-fashioneds with my corn flakes.*

domestic, *adj.* see **native.**

dull, *adj.* jejune: *Waiting till the sales are on to celebrate Christmas makes it rather jejune in January.* gormless: *Sidonia, who had read nothing since Mother Goose, just sat like a gormless fool while we discussed Areopagitica.*

dullard, *n.* see **bore.**

duty, *n.* dharma: *A visit to the aged parent is your dharma on Mother's Day.*

E

eager, *adj.* rath, rathe: *MacReady was a bit too rath to marry Tarantella, and now she's leading him a merry dance.*

eaglelike, *adj.* aquiline: *With her aquiline sight, Koringa saw her boyfriend when he was a mile away.*

earliness, *n.* (for a social engagement or date) prochronism: *Millicent! Because of your persistent prochronism you've caught me in the shower again.*

eastern, *adj.* oriental: *We tried to explain to Sean that flying from Shannon to Heathrow was hardly an oriental excursion.*

eat, *vb.* see **chew.**

eel-shaped, *adj.* anguilliform: *Hermione's anguilliform body was accentuated by her brief swimsuit.*

effeminate, *adj.* epicene: *Percy insisted there was nothing epicene in his wearing lace underwear.*

eloquent, *adj.* dithyrambic: *The critics received my latest novel with dithyrambic encomia.*

embezzle, *vb.* defalcate: *Fotheringay was defalcating the club funds, a mere peccadillo.* —**embezzlement,** *n.* defalcation.

embitter, *vb.* acerbate: *Refusing me my preprandial martini was the first act that acerbated me towards Proserpina.*

encouraging, *adj.* hortative, hortatory: *I thought that the beautiful blonde at the bar was giving me a hortatory signal, but the bartender explained that her nictitation was the result of a tic.*

enticement, *n.* gudgeon: *The stranger offered Suzie a sweet as a gudgeon to lure her to ride on his tricycle.*

equivocate, *vb.* tergiversate: *A firm adherent to girouettism, Cosmo Reed tergiversates on every issue from whom he should vote for to what bread he should buy.*

erstwhile, *adj.* see **former.**

everlasting, *adj.* aeonian: *Your aeonian nagging is driving me mad.*

excess, *n.* nimiety: *It would appear that Thimblewit is suffering from a nimiety of spirituous fluids.*

excitable, *adj.* (sexually excitable) erethismic, erethistic, erethitic: *All they have to do is say 'prunes' to make Virgil go off on an erethitic paroxysm of erotomania.*

extent, *n.* see **scope.**

extravagant, *adj.* sumptuary: *My weekly stipend of one shilling scarcely encouraged or gave much opportunity for sumptuary indulgences.*

encouraging, *adj.* hortative, hortatory: *I thought that the beautiful blonde at the bar was giving me a hortatory signal, but the bartender explained that her nictitation was the result of a tic.*

F

falsehood, *n.* see **lie.**

fanatic, *n.* zealot; energumen: *Alistair Ghurkin is an energumen when it comes to onychophagia.*

fatherlike, *adj.* patriclinous: *Patriclinous, filioclinous = 'Like father, like son.'*

fatness, *n.* see **stoutness.**

favourable, *adj.* dexter: *I overheard some dexter descants on my play in the theatre lobby.*

fearful, *adj.* pavid: *Don't be pavid, little girl, I just want to buy some of your violets.*

fearsome, *adj.* see **forbidding.**

femininity, *n.* muliebrity: *Phoebe complains that George's making her shoe the horses is an assault on her muliebrity.*

fishlike, *adj.* ichthyoid: *Between his anableptic eyes and his ichthyoid chin, Whelan looks like something washed up by the tide.*

fishy, *adj.* ichthyic: *How do you get your wife to believe that ichthyic tale about working late at the office every night?*

flabby, *adj.* quaggy: *A few sets of tennis every day will tighten up that quaggy gut.*

flag, *n.* guidon: *Ms. Rumplet is always waving the guidon for feminism.*

flammable, *adj.* ignescent: *Euphrenia's disposition is so ignescent that I'm afraid to tell her she's wearing her dress inside out.*

flattering, *adj.* gnathonic: *Frambesia's gym teacher had the most gnathonic comments about her performance at the swimming gala.* .

floating, *adj.* natant: *Waiter! There's a natant object in my martini!* supernatant: *There I was, my dear, supernatant in my life vest till carried ashore by a passing porpoise.*

flood, *n.* diluvium: *Mother, I'm afraid we've encountered a diluvial problem in the bathroom.* —**floodlike,** *adj.* diluvial.

flow, *vb.* (out) disembogue: *Water disembogued from three dolphins to fill the fountain.*

folly, *n.* bêtise: *The bêtise of lending money to Cadwallader is matched only by your money.*

fool, *n.* ninnyhammer: *When it comes to operating a computer, Algernon is just a gormless ninnyhammer.*

forbidding, *adj.* rebarbative: *I'd stay clear of Pfeffernüsse if I were you—he's a rebarbative tiddly-winks player.*

force, *vb.* dragoon: *I was dragooned into doing the washing-up last night.*

foreign-born, *adj.* allochthonous: *The allochthonous peoples of the United Kingdom often preserve their cultural heritages.*

forked, *adj.* furcate. (two-forked) bifurcate: *Proceed down this road, and keep left at the bifurcation.* —**furcation,** *n.*
—**bifurcation,** *n.*

former, *adj.* quondam: *Lothario's quondam cook used to spike his orange juice with Spanish fly.*

fortifying, *adj.* see **strengthening.**

foul-smelling, *adj.* see **putrid.**

four-colour, *adj.* tetrachromatic: *Our agency has run our tetrachromatic advert in the Sunday magazine.* —(something) **four-coloured,** *n.* tetrachrome.

foursome, *n.* quaternity: *I'm trying to organize a quaternity for bridge.*

fragments, *n. pl.* disjecta membra: *I tried, after the divorce, to pick up the disjecta membra of my sex life.*

freckled, *adj.* macular: *I merely told her that I liked her macular face, and she stamped off.* —**macula,** *n.*

friendly, *adj.* avuncular: *The army cadets were immediately made to feel comfortable by Sergeant Grunt's avuncular warmth.*

funnel-shaped, *adj.* infundibular, infundibuliform: *I've always been rather fond of the infundibuliform nose and hat of the Tin Woodman in* The Wonderful Wizard of Oz.

G

gap, *n.* lacuna (*pl.* lacunae): *There is a noticeable lacuna in this censored version of* Tropic of Cancer, *by Henry Miller.* diastema: *The voyeurs were peering into the nudist camp through a diastema in the fence.*

gaping, *adj.* see **open-mouthed.**

garden, *n.* garth: *Mrs. Thumble could be found, of an evening, quietly resting in her garth, sipping gin through a straw.*

gardener, *n.* (lawn maintenance) agrostologist: *Our agrostologist comes once a week with two assistants.*

garliclike, *adj.* alliaceous: *The third-class carriage on the Rome-Florence express had an alliaceous air about it.*

gathered, *adj.* agminate: *As usual, the agminate free-loaders could be found at the beer keg at the company outing.*

gay, *adj.* galliard: *Oh, didn't we have a galliard time in the good old days!*

generosity, *adj.* munificence: *Owing to the munificence of our benefactor, Ronald Pinchbeck, the Society will now be able to afford a dandelion border in the flowerbeds.*

gentle, *adj.* mansuetudinous: *The slave driver in the galley was most mansuetudinous: he gave us the lash only once every hour.*
—**mansuetude,** *n.*

gardener, *n.* (lawn maintenance) agrostologist:
*Our agrostologist comes once a week with two
assistants.*

genuine, *adj.* (Ger.) echt: *Bibi's dentist assured me that her teeth are echt—something I'd expected ever since she put the bite on me for a loan.*

gibberish, *n.* galimatias: *This paper, Snidely, is the worst gallimaufry of galimatias I've ever seen!*

gluttony, *n.* gulosity: *It was hard to convince Chester Gombaul that gulosity is one of the seven deadly sins.*

goodbye, *adj.* apopemptic: *We paid our apopemptic respects to the host and hostess and went home.*

gossipmonger, *n.* quidnunc: *You'd best not tell Nellie Shamble that you short-circuited your vibrator—he's such a quidnunc it'll be around the club in a day.*

granular, *adj.* grumous: *Eating dry biscuits in bed always gives me a somewhat grumous feeling.*

grapelike, *adj.* botryoidal, botryose: *The epergne, consisting of a botryoidal cluster of painted ping-pong balls, added a certain* je ne sais quoi *to the decor.*

grass-eating, *adj.* graminivorous: *Having been a vegetarian for several years, Miss Grimple decided to specialize, and she's now strictly graminivorous.*

grasslike, *adj.* gramineous: *The hula-hula dancers were uniformly attired in gramineous garments which left them bare-waisted up to the neck.*

grass-eating, *adj.* graminivorous: *Having been a vegetarian for several years, Miss Grimple decided to specialize, and she's now strictly graminivorous.*

greedy, *adj.* esurient; edacious: *The wedding guests demonstrated their edacity by consuming everything in sight, including the plaster bride and groom on the cake.* —**edacity,** *n.* See also **gluttony.**

gritty, *adj.* see **sandy.**

guide, *n.* dragoman; Cicerone: *Our dragoman at the museum was a lovely Japanese girl.*

H

hag, *n.* beldam: *The beldam in charge of the door denied us entrance till we had given her baksheesh.*

hairy, *adj.* hispid: *Twerker was really turned on by Rosanna's hispid upper lip.*

half, *n.* moiety: *The trouble is that Shypoke will want a moiety of the profits if he does all the work.*

halve, *vb.* dimidiate: *Inflation has all but dimidiated my salary, and I must have an increase, Mr. Barfwell.*

hanging, *n.* see **tapestry.**

happiness, *n.* eudemonia: *Eudemonia is a calefacient canine.* —**eudemonic,** *adj.*

harmful, *adj.* nocent; nocuous; noxious: *Failing to pay that gambling debt may be noxious to your health.* mephitic: *The mephitic odours wafting from your pot au feu make me wonder if your kitchen hasn't been checked out by the shadow minister for the environment.* malefic: *It was downright malefic of Winklepowder to send his teacher a condolence card—she wasn't even ill.*

harmless, *adj.* innocuous: *My ancient car has fallen into innocuous desuetude.*

hatchet-shaped, *adj.* dolabriform: *The dowager's dolabriform profile belied her gentle nature.*

hawklike, *adj.* accipitrine: *The politician's accipitrine views of the foreign situation were in sharp contrast to the columbine attitudes of his colleagues.*

headless, *adj.* see **leaderless.**

healthy, *adj.* salubrious: *The natives offered us a most salubrious repast of cooked insects, which we politely declined.*

henchman, *n.* myrmidon: *The tax collector arrived with two myrmidons, so I had to pay up.*

henlike, *adj.* gallinaceous: *The party is strictly a gallinaceous affair.*

hiccup, *n.* singultus: *We could hardly understand Comrade Pisovski's speech because it was punctuated here and there with a loud singultus.*

hooflike, *adj.* ungular: *If he doesn't behave himself, I shall apply my ungular extremity to his gluteus maximus.*

horny, *adj.* keratoid: *The ecdysiast had a keratoid effect on the audience.*

hot-tempered, *adj.* sulphurous: *Scheisskopf's sulphurous nature did not recommend him for being a magistrate.*

hourly, *adj.* horal: *The police claimed that if the prostitutes walked round the square once every hour, they were chargeable with horal turpitude.*

hunger, *n.* (insatiable hunger) bulimia: *Mr. Thwock's bulimia for stewed prunes has continued unabated.* See also **mania.**

hunting, *n.* venery: *Lord Humpington has gone off into the forest to engage in venery with Lady Humpington.*

I

ideal, *n.* apotheosis: *Ethel Titmarsh was the apotheosis of womanhood to Mr. Flogbottom.*

ignoramus, *n.* see **fool.**

hunting, *n.* venery: *Lord Humpington has gone off into the forest to engage in venery with Lady Humpington.*

ignorant, *adj.* nescient: *The pinheaded nescience exhibited by the amateur chefs at the bake-off was matched only by their gulosity.*
   —**ignorance,** *n.* nescience.

ill-at-ease, *adj.* dysphoric: *You don't have to feel dysphoric with me, young man.*

imitator, *n.* epigone: *Philibeg Krotch has had many epigones as a writer but no equals.*

implore, *vb.* obtest; obsecrate: *If you want something, don't obsecrate me for it, just ask.*

impudent, *adj.* malapert: *That malapert young puppy has smeared glue on my monocle!*

inconvenience, *vb.* discommode: *I found the lack of toilet paper quite discommoding.*

indecent, *adj.* scabrous: *Harlotta's mother tells such scabrous stories at dinner that we avoid inviting her.*

indifference, *n.* accidie: *Her accidie towards everything I do gives a hint why she won't go out with me.*

indifferent, *adj.* laodicean: *Alphonse said he was entirely laodicean as regards your attending his third birthday party.*

indisputable, *adj.* see **undeniable.**

ineffective, *adj.* adiaphorous: *Sweeney is the most adiaphorous salesman on the staff.*

inescapable, *adj.* ineluctable: *That the Countess Silenzia is an inarticulate thimblewit is an ineluctable conclusion drawn after two minutes in her presence.*

41

ineffective, *adj.* adiaphorous: *Sweeney is the most adiaphorous salesman on the staff.*

inflexible, *adj.* renitent: *Josiah Mingent was renitent in his rule that everyone attending his daughter Retro's wedding reception had to bring a gift.*

insane, *adj.* mattoid: *Odd as it may seem, Hempenfinger's predilection for eating live goldfish was not regarded as particularly mattoid in his circle.*

inside out, evaginate: *Your pullover is evaginate.*

insincere, *adj.* meretricious: *Mercator accused his wife of being meretricious when she expressed interest in his projection.*

insomniac, *adj.* agrypnotic: *I spent an agrypnotic night at Sonia's last week.*

inspiration, *n.* afflatus: *Whenever Throckmorton felt an afflatus coming on, everyone would leave the room.*

interpreter, *n.* (of recondite arcana) hierophant. See **interpretive.**

interpretive, *adj.* hermeneutic: *Explication of the Inland Revenue regulations requires a hermeneutic hierophant in advanced trivia.*

intersect, *vb.* (in giving a tourist directions) decussate: *You drive about a mile to where the roads decussate. . . .*

intestinal, *adj.* alvine: *Fresser's persistent interprandial consumption reflects his alvine preoccupation.*

intricate, *adj.* gongoristic; anfractuous: *The politician's campaign speech was representative of his anfractuous thinking.*

inspiration, *n.* afflatus: *Whenever Throckmorton felt an afflatus coming on, everyone would leave the room.*

invigorating, *adj.* analeptic: *Seeing you again was certainly analeptic.*

irrelevant, *adj.* aliunde: *One can always count on Mrs. Flib to contribute some aliunde remarks at the dinner table.*

irritable, *adj.* iracund: *Theodosia's iracund nature did little to endear her to her acquaintances.* atrabilious: *Any adverse critique of this book will be written by an atrabilious, adiaphorous dolt.*

J

jalopy, *n.* shandrydan: *Pindar Fleet picked up Lottie in his shandrydan to go to the races.*

K

kiss, *n.* bilabial click: *Sonora Vimble collected little money at the bazaar where she had a booth selling bilabial clicks for charity.*

knife, *n.* (E. Africa) panga; (Borneo) parang: *He took out his parang and made short work of his attackers.*

L

lakeshore, *n.* lacustrine: *We enjoy a lacustrine holiday each year in Switzerland.*

lament, *n.* jeremiad: *We were forced to listen to Mrs. Grumble's interminable jeremiad about the lateness of the train.*

lascivious, *adj.* see **lustful.**

lateness, *n.* (for a social engagement or date) parachronism: *As usual, Bridget, your parachronism has caused us to miss the first act.*

laugh, *vb.* cachinnate: *The raucous cachinnation emanating from the next room prevented me from sleeping.* —**cachinnation,** *n.*

laughing, *adj.* rident: *Archibald Klump's rident spirit buoyed us up while we drifted in the life raft.*

lazy, *adj.* otiose; oscitant: *Kiki Grindelwasser was so oscitant she had to have artificial respiration.* —**oscitancy, oscitance, oscitation,** *n.*

leaderless, *adj.* acephalous: *When the president resigned, our company was acephalous for several months.*

lethargy, *n.* hebetude: *Wrigglestaff's lethargy is fortunately punctuated by an occasional palpebration, so we know he's alive.*

letter, *n.* epistle; missive: *I hope that in her memoirs Lovelia isn't planning to reveal the contents of the missives I sent her—most of them were rather rude mash notes.*

lewdness, *n.* lubricity: *How can you be so sure that Sir John's acts of lubricity are confined to restrooms in deserted railway stations?* —**lubricous, lubricious,** *adj.*

lie, *n.* mendacity: *Just because we exchanged vests, it is a mendacity to call us transvestites.* —**mendacious,** *adj.*

liniment, *n.* see **lotion.**

link, *n.* nexus: *There may be a nexus between the missing money and Arthur's new car.*

lively, *adj.* see **gay.**

long-legged, *adj.* grallatorial: *The show-girls in Las Vegas are certainly grallatorial.*

lotion, *n.* embrocation: *The doctor said he'd never heard of using warm beer as an embrocation.*

lousy, *adj.* pedicular: *I try to avoid those places where pedicular people congregate.*

lustful, *adj.* randy; goatish; lecherous; ruttish; caprine; rammish; hircine: *Harrigan's hircine habits don't make him a popular guest at sweet-16 parties.*

47

M

magic, *n.* sortilege: *Nefertiti Buttonweiser practised her sortilege on any man who came within reach.*

man-hater, *n.* misanthrope: *Frances Veverrine is not really such a feminist—she's merely a misanthrope.*

mania, *n.* cacoethes: *At the age of 78, Mrs. Phrogg developed a cacoethes for mountain-climbing.* See also **hunger.**

manifestation, *n.* avatar: *Cornelia is the avatar of Philip's wildest fantasies about women.*

manoeuvre, *n.* (diplomatic) démarche: *Assassinating the Duke at Sarajevo was not exactly the démarche of the century.*

marshy, *adj.* paludal: *They sat round the campfire, toasting paludal mallows.*

mate, *vb.* (random mating) panmixia, panmixis: *The invitation to this party mentioned nothing about panmixia.*

materialistic, *adj.* see **mechanical.**

mattress, *n.* palliasse: *Get your bally arse off my palliasse.* Also, paillasse: *Get your pale arse off my paillasse.*

meagre, *adj.* exiguous: *She's so extravagant that she can hardly get along on her exiguous income of £500,000 a year.*

mechanical, *adj.* banausic: *Frimkin's banausic instincts made him gravitate to the wealthy and influential.*

man-hater, *n.* misanthrope: *Frances Veverrine is not really such a feminist—she's merely a misanthrope.*

mediator, *n.* paraclete: *After the knock-down, the paraclete ordered the boxer into a neutral corner.*

medical, *adj.* iatric: *My darling son, Eustace, completes his iatric education next spring; afterwards he'll be a locum as witch doctor to the Goomba tribe in Ghana.*

memory, *n.* see **recollection.**

messy, *adj.* see **unkempt.**

mild, *adj.* see **gentle.**

minty, *adj.* menthaceous: *Would you like a menthaceous postprandial chocolate?*

mischief, *n.* diablerie: *The boys were engaged in a bit of diablerie behind the barn with the milkmaids.*

misconduct, *n.* malversation: *No, Cranshaw, you cannot sue a phrenologist for malversation because he found a bump that indicated you were litigious.*

misplacement, *n.* (geographic) anachorism: *Suggesting that Hawkhurst is in Tierra del Fuego is pure anachorism.* (chronological) anachronism: *Claiming that Milton was Shakespeare's mother is a good example of anachronism.*

mispronunciation, *n.* cacoepy: *Many bad puns are the result of cacoepy.* —cacoepistic, *adj.*

misspelling, *n.* cacography: *The N.Y. Times seems to prefer the cacographic form "millenium."* —cacographic, *adj.*

mixture, *n.* macedoine: *The street was littered with a macedoine of sweets and chewing-gum wrappers, dirty paper cups, and torn newspapers.*

model, *n.* paradigm; paragon: *Sophonisba was a paradigm of virtue.*

modest, *adj.* see **shy.**

mouldy, adj. mucid: *From the mucid vapours arising from that pair of socks, I'd guess they're yours, Musgrave.*

mournful, *adj.* lugubrious: *No, Wamble, the Marquis de Sade was not so named because he was the most lugubrious chap in town.*

multisyllabic, *adj.* sesquipedalian: *Eva Scuttle delights in confusing her husband by lacing her speech with sesquipedalian confusibles.*

murmur, *vb.* see **sigh, whisper.**

musty, *adj.* see **mouldy.**

mysterious, *adj.* numinous: *Fifi was bathed in a numinous scent that had an aphrodisiac effect on Aurangzeb.*

mystery, *n. (pl.* **mysteries)** arcana: *Only the highest officials were familiar with the arcana of Pipistrella's award of a Ph.D. at Cambridge.*

mouldy, *adj.* mucid: *From the mucid vapours arising from that pair of socks, I'd guess they're yours, Musgrave.*

N

nag, *n.* shrew; harridan; termagant: *Twilby has married Gonforth's widow, an old termagant if I ever saw one.*

naive, *adj.* jejune: *It's rather jejune of Harnischfeger to believe that women are after him because of his name.*

native, *adj.* autochthonous: *The wild life autochthonous to Honoria's kitchen included ants, mice, and cockroaches.* enchorial: *The enchorial practice of eating visitors has discouraged the emergence of New Guinea as a tourist mecca.*

nearing, *adj.* see **approaching.**

new, *adj.* neoteric: *Lord Farthingale's neoteric interest is phillumeny.*

nodding, *adj.* nutational: *We have a nutational acquaintance—he means nodding to me and I mean nodding to him.*

nonnative, *n.* (Maori) pakeha: *This place becomes livable after the pakehas clear out at the end of the summer.*

nonsense, *n.* see **gibberish.**

nonsensical, *adj.* amphigoric: *American advertising provides a never-ending source of amphigoric writing.*

northern, *adj.* boreal: *Winter arrived with an icy, boreal blast.*

nosebleed, *n.* epistaxis: *Carmine Foon had been warned that insulting people could lead to ecchymosis and epistaxis.*

O

obesity, *n.* see **stoutness.**

obligatory, *adj.* deontic: *Prompt payment of your club dues is deontic.*

obscure, *vb.* adumbrate; obnubilate: *Vivian Trembly's eyes were all but obnubilated by a shock of pink hair.* —Delphic, *adj.: The ratiocination behind Adolf's predilection for wearing silk underwear is somewhat Delphic.* —(of literary style) **Gongorism,** *n.*

offal, *n.* (of fish) gurry: *Sandra Gecko invited me for an Indian dinner and I swear she served gurry curry.*

offset, *vb.* equiponderate: *Thrilby's edacity is somewhat equiponderated by his edentulous condition.*

ogle, *n.* oeillade: *Felucca Kleinschmidt delighted in every oeillade made at her while she served behind the bar at the Dog and Duck.*

onionlike, *adj.* see **garliclike.**

open-mouthed, *adj.* patulous; rictal: *We gazed in rictal astonishment as Katinka lifted the car so we could change the tyre.*

opaque, *vb.* devitrify: *The more he explained, the more devitrified his argument became.*

opposite, *adj.* antipodal, antipodean: *Rubella's antiphon to Egbert's proposition was antipodean to that of Maud.*

optimistic, *adj.* taurine: *Kurt Knoedelscheiss will never make any money in the Stock Market —one day he's taurine, the next, ursine.*

oral, *adj.* buccal: *Frisbie's buccal breeze was redolent with alliaceous halitosis.*

ornate, *adj.* (of language) florid; aureate: *Councillor O'Leake was known for his aureate oratorical style.*

ostrichlike, *adj.* struthious: *Your struthious attitude won't make the naughty man go away.*

outburst, *n.* ebullition: *'I never expected such an ebullition of emotion from Fanny when I told her I was pregnant,' said George.*

outline, *vb.* adumbrate: *Your adumbration of the plan has made it pellucid for me.*

overabundance, *n.* nimiety: *It's a pity, but there appears to be a nimiety of gormless microcephalics in that organization.*

overlapping, *adj.* imbricate: *It's not nice, Moncrieff, to say 'I like that imbricate look' to someone who has shingles.*

oxlike, *adj.* see **cowlike.**

overabundance, *n.* nimiety: *It's a pity, but there appears to be a nimiety of gormless microcephalics in that organization.*

P

painful, *adj.* nociceptive: *Fremdwort's love affair with the widow Sneckpiff was a most nociceptive interlude.*

pan-shaped, *adj.* patellate: *His patellate face gives me the creeps.*

parasitic, *adj.* (worm) helminth: *Niminy—the helminth—has borrowed money from everyone, including his five-year-old niece.* autecious: *Oscar's relationship with his friends has always been an autecious one.* —**helminthic,** *adj.*

patience, *n.* longanimity: *Humperdinck waited so long at the brothel that he almost exhausted his longanimity.*

payment, *n.* see **reward.**

peacocklike, *adj.* pavonine: *Farfanella's pavonine behaviour was just to show off her new dress.*

peel, *vb.* decorticate: *Decorticate a grape for me, would you, Darling?* desquamate: *Keep your eyes desquamated in case the beadle comes by.*

perishableness, *n.* caducity: *The caducity of Professor Hedgeline's novels makes one wonder why he bothers writing them at all.*

perplex, *vb.* see **bewilder.**

perquisite, *n.* appanage: *These days, the two-hour coffee breaks, morning and afternoon, as well as two-hour lunch breaks have become the standard appanage of many jobs.*

persecute, *vb.* dragonnade: *Oh, Susan! Why must you dragonnade me with your dulcet doits?*

person, *n.* gowk: *Ms. Anne Thropy is a pagurian gowk.*

pessimistic, *adj.* ursine: *Ursula Klutz has sold all her shares in IBM because of an ursine feeling.*

pin-headed, *adj.* microcephalic: *Of all the microcephalic things to do, Sneckthwaite, putting ice in one's beer ranks among the dumbest.*

pitted, *adj.* scrobiculate: *Hempelfinger's scrobiculate complexion looks like the surface of the moon.*

playing-field, *n.* (in Malaya) padang: *Heroes are made on the padangs of Eton.*

pliant, *adj.* sequacious: *Leonidas Piffle is scarcely a strong candidate for election to the council —he's too sequacious and he's a girouettist, besides.*

plumpness, *n.* see **stoutness.**

pointed, *adj.* (two-pointed) bicuspidate: *Since he's twice as stupid as anyone else I know, I'm not surprised at his bicuspidate head.* aculeate: *Fenwick Grendel is known for his aculeate remarks.* mucronate: *I suppose that the idea of having a flag-pole-sitting party came out of your mucronate head.*

pollute, *vb.* maculate: *Old Knoedelwasser has been maculating our drinking water again.* —maculation, *n.*

polysyllabic, *adj.* see **multisyllabic.**

pompous, *adj.* orotund: *The MP's orotund manner of addressing constituents lost him many votes.*

poppylike *n.* papaveraceous: *The odour from that pipe of yours indicates papaveraceous contents.*

popular, *adj.* demotic: *Phiebelphinger's treatise on flyspecks was not the demotic success he'd expected.*

positive, *adj.* see **arbitrary.**

pouch-shaped, *adj.* bursiform: *Mrs. Plote's bursiform cheeks were rubicund with embarrassment.*

poverty-stricken, *adj.* indigent; necessitous: *My necessitous condition earned me little sympathy on Skid Row.*

praiseworthy, *adj.* palmary: *A palmary performance on the gut-bucket won a music scholarship for my niece, Cleopatra.*

precious, *adj.* alembicated: *Gattopardo's alembicated style makes his books hard to read.*

principle, *n.* numen (*pl.* numina): *Pickstaff's numen is the first part of the three musketeers' motto —'All for one'—provided that he's the one.*

problem, *n.* nodus: *Getting free seats for Wimbledon may prove a bit of a nodus, Hackluyt.*

prompt, *adj.* see **eager.**

prone, *adj.* decumbent: *Farfula was decumbent on the grass, reading a book.*

poppylike *n.* papaveraceous: *The odour from that pipe of yours indicates papaveraceous contents.*

protrude, *vb.* exsert: *Their lips exserted, then met in a prolonged encounter.*

proud, *adj.* orgulous: *You should be orgulous about your acclaim as a virtuoso on the ocarina.*

publicity, *n.* réclame: *Its inventor has never received the réclame he deserved for inventing the fly swatter.*

purify, *vb.* depurate; despumate: *Waiter, has this water been despumated?*

putrid, *adj.* mephitic: *The mephitic fetor arising from your gym socks is more than I can stand.*

quick, *adj.* (quick-witted) tachyencephalic, tachyencephalous: *Ogilvie's tachyencephalous response to the comedian's insult was to give him the finger.*

R

radiant, *adj.* lambent; effulgent: *The cat's eyes were effulgent in the dark.*

radiating, *adj.* quaquaversal: *We soon discovered that the quaquaversal odour emanated from Carbottle's feet.*

rainy, *adj.* hyetal: *There was a hyetal interruption of the picnic, but the edacious guests soon returned to the business of the gavage.*

rapidly, *adv.* tantivy: *Frobisher Piklok ran tantivy for his car the instant the alarm was set off.*

rare, *adj.* see **choice.**

real, *adj.* see **genuine.**

rebel, *n.* recusant: *Frobisher, a recusant all the way, refused to genuflect when the sergeant entered the barracks.*

reclusive, *adj.* (and cranky) pagurian: *Barfinger's pagurian ways did little to endear him to his neighbours.*

recollection, *n.* anamnesis: *Although Barnaby Grudge was 90, his anamnesis was totally unimpaired.*

recur, *vb.* recrudesce: *We all thought that Dupetschky had got rid of his foul manners, but they recrudesced last night at the plumbers' ball.*

reedlike, *adj.* arundinaceous: *Between his arachnoid legs and his arundinaceous body, Frobisher did not cut an impressive figure in his ballet tights.*

radiating, *adj.* quaquaversal: *We soon discovered
that the quaquaversal odour emanated from
Carbottle's feet.*

refined, *adj.* see **precious.**

refuse, *n.* recrement: *They used to call them dustmen or garbagemen, then sanitationmen, and now they refer to them as recrement collectors.*

reiterate, *vb.* see **repeat.**

related, *adj.* agnate: *Even though we are both named Jim Smith, we are not agnate in any way.*

relaxed, *adj.* dégagé: *Smedley was so dégagé in his chair that we felt his pulse to make sure he was alive.*

repeat, *vb.* ingeminate: *Nolan can't recall at what age he no longer paid attention to the oft-ingeminated warning that he would become a sissy if he played with girls.*

reply, *n.* see **answer.**

response, *n.* see **answer.**

resuscitation, *n.* anabiosis: *All efforts to effect anabiosis of Coryander Gluck proved fruitless.*

reward, *n.* guerdon: *As a token guerdon for his 50 years of faithful service, the board decided to give Havering a box of exploding cigars, not aware that he'd given up smoking.*

ridicule, *vb.* pasquinade: *In Nazi Germany, it was considered rather bad form to pasquinade Heinrich Himmler.*

rod-shaped, *adj.* baculiform, bacilliform: *Keep your bacilliform digits to yourself.*

relaxed, *adj.* dégagé: *Smedley was so dégagé in his chair that we felt his pulse to make sure he was alive.*

roll, *n.* obvolution: *Mr. Big peeled a large denomination note from his obvolution and gave it to the lavatory attendant.*

rotgut, *n.* (rotgut brandy) aguardiente (lit. 'firewater'): *After dinner, all the guests were treated to large snifters of the host's homemade aguardiente.*

roundabout, *adj.* ambagious: *Sophronia's perpetual excuse that she had to wash her hair is nothing more than an ambagious way of refusing to go out with Archibald.* See also **intricate.**

rubbish, *n.* gangue: *The dustman considers gangue to be a collectible.*

rude, *adj.* see **uncouth.**

rumbling, (of the stomach) borborygmus: *In a momentary silence, the after-dinner speaker's borborygmic thunderings echoed throughout the hall.* —**borborygmal, borborygmic,** *adj.*

rural, *adj.* see **rustic.**

rustic, *adj.* villatic: *Yes, Binker, I shall retire and live out my life in villatic simplicity in Tierra del Fuego.* See also **uncouth.**

S

sad, *adj.* lachrymose: *Everyone in the airport stopped to watch Schlumberger's lachrymose farewells to his pet frog.*

salary, *n.* emolument: *Mr. Gringsby pretended he didn't understand when I asked him for an increase in my emolument.*

sandy, *adj.* arenose; sabulose; sabulous: *I'm not sure the waiter understood you, Dr. Johnson, when you told him your oysters were sabulous.* —**sabulosity,** *n.*

sarcastic, *adj.* mordacious: *Caldwell resents any mordacious remarks made about his new skirt and pumps.*

sausage-shaped, *adj.* allantoid: *His allantoid fingers do not help to make Finnegan an expert watchmaker.*

scanty, *adj.* see **meagre.**

scatter, *vb.* disject: *The family was disjected to the four corners of the earth.* (scattered members) disjecta membra.

scimitar-shaped, *adj.* acinaciform: *Miss Thwick's acinaciform nose was her most distinctive feature.*

scold, *vb.* objurgate: *Feistinella is always objurgating her husband for wearing black socks in bed.*

scope, *n.* ambit: *The ambit of the government's report on the nesting habits of the roc was very limited.*

scram!, *interj.* aroint thee!: *'Aroint thee, witch!'*
the rump-fed runyon cried.

scraping, *adj.* rasorial: *With inflation the way it*
is, one must be downright rasorial just to get
by.

seashore, *n., adj.* littoral: *Do you prefer a*
lacustrine or a littoral holiday?

secret, *adj.* cabbalistic: *We were initiated into the*
club in a series of cabbalistic rites.

secrets, *n. pl.* penetralia: *Bascombe, a former*
C.I.A. agent, refused to reveal his penetralia to
his wife.

self-discipline, *n.* ascesis: *Only through a severe*
programme of ascesis was Papilio able to stop biting
his toenails.

semblance, *n.* simulacrum *(pl.* simulacra): *Since*
her bout with the flu, Bombastina has been a
mere simulacrum of her robust self.

senility, *n.* dotage; caducity: *I am not convinced*
that Sherman's cachectic behaviour at the age
of 35 can be ascribed to caducity.

separate, *vb.* decollate: *One must decollate the*
wheat from the chaff. (separation) *n.*
decollation: *After decollation of the forms,*
send one copy to me and the other to the
Inland Revenue. diastasis: *My wife and I have*
arranged a temporary diastasis.

servant, *n.* (boy) gossoon: *I say there, gossoon,*
may I have a glass of water.

shadowy, *adj.* tenebrous: *Sapolio's past is*
somewhat tenebrous—he was once a
lexicographer.

self-discipline, *n.* ascesis: *Only through a severe programme of ascesis was Papilio able to stop biting his toenails.*

shady, *adj.* umbrageous: *Melisande is going out with some umbrageous buffoon who claims to make his living as a birdwatcher.*

sharp, *adj.* see **cutting.**

sharp-eyed, *adj.* lyncean: *It didn't require the lyncean talents of the lookout to tell us we had struck an iceberg.*

shave, *vb.* depilate: *I had a thought while I was depilating this morning.*

shed, *vb.* exuviate: *Everyone cheered when the ecdysiast exuviated her clothing atop the bar.*

sheeplike, *adj.* ovine: *Lt. Thimble's ovine behaviour imparted little confidence to the men he was leading into battle.*

shifty, *adj.* louche: *If you don't agree that Farfella has a louche character, then how do you explain her nightly earnings from playing poker in Piccadilly.*

shining, *adj.* see **bright.**

shrew, *n.* termagant; marabunta; maenad: *Major Flews considers all women to be termagants, maenads, and marabuntas.*

shy, *adj.* verecund: *Aspodilla is so verecund that on her nuptial night she retired fully clothed.*

sigh, *vb.* suspire; sough: *Sophie soughed softly as Stephen served the soufflé.*

silent, *adj.* obmutescent: *Olga always liked the brawny, obmutescent type, so I can't understand why she married Oswald Nancy.*

sceptic, *n.* nullifidian: *I confess I'm a nullifidian when you tell me about having travelled in a flying saucer.*

slander, *vb.* vilipend: *These days, a female parent may consider herself vilipended by being called 'Mother'.*

slavery, *n.* dulosis; helotism: *He was the first gangster ever heard to refer to white slavery as 'etiolated dulosis'.*

sleepy, *adj.* narcoleptic: *The speech was so dull that I at once succumbed to a narcoleptic state.*

slight, *vb.* disoblige: *Chauncy felt a bit disobliged by Queenie's disaffirmation of his privileges.*

slimy, *adj.* mucid: *Fianciulla Ginsberg keeps that mucid snake in her bathtub.*

slow, *adj.* (slow-witted) bradyencephalic, bradyencephalous: *Finster is bradyencephalous —but reliable.*

slowing, *adj.* ritenuto; ritardando; rallentando: *I've noticed a rallentando reaction in the Major lately—he's down to a half bottle of port a night.*

smooth, *adj.* levigate: *The baby's levigate bottom reminds me of his father's glabrous dome.*

snake, *n.* fer-de-lance: *She turned and gave me a questioning glance / As I fingered the tip of my fer-de-lance.*

snakelike, *adj.* anguine: *Eustace was attracted by Fifi's anguine charms.*

sneeze, *vb.* sternutate: *Look here, Pinocchio, hay fever is no excuse for sternutating in my soup!*

71

sneeze, *vb.* sternutate: *Look here, Pinocchio, hay fever is no excuse for sternutating in my soup!*

snowy, *adj.* niveous: *Under that niveous mane dwelt a brain the size of a pea.*

soapy, *adj.* saponaceous: *Lulu, I do wish you would perform your saponaceous ablutions before dinner.*

soften, *vb.* detumesce: *You shouldn't eat a peach till it has detumesced.* (softening) *n.* detumescence: *Jennifer noted a marked detumescence in Reggie's attitude by the end of the evening.*

soothing, *adj.* lenitive: *After I stubbed my toe, I was about to succumb to the podiatrist's lenitive ministrations when I realized that he was a foot-fetishist.*

sorcery, *n.* magic.

sour, *adj.* verjuice, verjuiced: *That teratoid verjuiced termagant whom Butch married won't let him out to go drinking.*

southern, *adj.* austral: *An austral breeze rippled the surface of Fimkin's martini.*

spidery, *adj.* arachnoid: *With his arachnoid legs, Arthur Twomble should never have taken up ballet.*

spiny, *adj.* aculeate; acanthoid: *Our dog had an acanthoid encounter with a porcupine.* See also **bristly.**

spiral, *adj.* (left to right) dextrorse; (right to left) sinistrorse: *Is that new staircase you installed dextrorse or sinistrorse?*

split, *vb.* dichotomize: *Your trousers have dichotomized at the seat.* —**dichotomy,** *n.*

spot, *vb.* see **pollute.**

spreading, *adj.* patulous: *Wipe that patulous grin off your face.*

starchlike, *adj.* amyloid: *The nuns could be identified by their amyloid habits.*

stench, *n.* effluvium: *The mephitic effluvium that emanated from Carpathia's lips drove some men wild.*

stinglike, *adj.* aculeate: *Keep your aculeate nose out of my affairs!*

storehouse, *n.* godown: *Omphalosceptics regard the navel as the godown of intelligence.*

stoutness, *n.* embonpoint: *Felicity's embonpoint made her a somewhat less than likely choice to play Peter Pan.*

strengthening, *adj.* roborant: *At the end of the race, the yachtsmen did not regard warm milk as a particularly roborant potion.*

strip, *vb.* see **shed.**

striped, *adj.* bayadère: *We all thought that Mrs. Rumbottom's bayadère T-shirt was very fetching.*

student, *n.* (drunken) goliard: *The Master disapproved of galliard goliards attending the college garden-party.*

stuff, *vb.* gavage: *The gulosity of the guests engaged in gavaging was simply gorgeous.*

stupid, *adj.* see **dull.**

summer, *vb.* aestivate: *We shall be aestivating on the Riviera next year.*

summerlike, *adj.* aestival: *My plans for an aestival holiday have not yet been made.*

sunset, *n.* (occurring at sunset) acronical: *Sidonie has an acronical predisposition towards sex.*

susceptible, *adj.* diathetic: *Phoebe is so terribly diathetic to men.* —**diathesis,** *n.*

swallowing, *n.* deglutition: *Too rapid deglutition can lead to dyspepsia.*

sweat, *n.* (foul-smelling) bromhidrosis; osmidrosis: *Eulalia didn't work Thesmond too hard because she couldn't abide his osmidrosis.*

swelling, *adj.* see **bulging.**

swimming, *adj.* see **floating.**

swimming pool, *n.* natatorium: *A few fast laps in the natatorium at dawn every day should whet your appetite for breakfast.*

swindle, *vb.* see **cheat.**

swollen, *adj.* incrassate: *See there? My ear is incrassate where Gloria bit it.*

T

tailless, *adj.* ecaudate; excaudate: *The definition of human being as an excaudate, featherless biped seems somehow inadequate.*

talkative, *adj.* logorrheic: *At dinner I was subjected to so much logorrheic bombast by Colonel Frumple that I fell asleep and missed dessert.* —**logorrhea,** *n.*

tapestry, *n.* arras: *Hamlet stabbed Polonius through the arras.*

tearful, *adj.* see **sad.**

tenderize, *vb.* intenerate: *You dolt! I said to intenerate the steak, not incinerate it!*

thick-headed, *adj.* hebetudinous: *Thirly's so hebetudinous he practically needs artificial respiration to keep breathing.*

thoughtless, *adj.* incogitant: *A nosegay of roses is an incogitant gift for someone with rose fever.*

threatening, *adj.* minacious, minatory, minatorial: *Mr. Piminy, who was about to pinch the waitress, was stopped by a minacious look from his wife.*

thunderous, *adj.* brontoid: *Quirt's brontoid whispering could be heard throughout the library.*

timid, *adj.* see **afraid.**

tip, *n.* douceur; baksheesh: *These days, a porter expects baksheesh just for telling you the right time.*

tiptoe, *adj.* (on tiptoe) digitigrade: *His digitigrade passage through the corridor did not waken his mother.*

toadying, *adj.* sycophantic; gnathonic: *That gnathonic oaf, Nehemiah Mincing, will never get anywhere offering steak dinners to Siegfried —he's a vegetarian.*

toothless, *adj.* edentate; edentulous: *That edentulous hussy made a pass at my husband!*

tramp, *n.* see **beggar.**

tranquillizing, *adj.* see **calming.**

transparent, *adj.* hyaline: *Gregory Humph's excuse for leaving was hyaline—we all knew he wasn't allowed out after eight at night.*

treatise, *n.* pandect: *All we did was ask the way to the men's room and the manager delivered himself of a pandect on the architecture of the hotel.*

trifle, *n.* doit; bagatelle; quelquechose: *That Rolls I gave you, my dear, is a mere bagatelle, a quelquechose that hints at my affection for you.*

trifling, *adj.* nugatory: *The maître d'hôtel offered us some nugatory chocolates after dinner.*

trite, *adj.* bathetic: *Postman's bathetic style will never win him a Nobel prize for literature.*

true, *adj.* apodictic: *Everything I told my wife about where I spent last night was apodictic.*

tuft, *n.* panicle: *Hugh Festerly is a veritable Nimrod among the panicle-hunters.*

toothless, *adj.* edentate; edentulous: *That edentulous hussy made a pass at my husband!*

tufted, *adj.* (densely tufted) cespitose: *Hortense Quagmeyer did not find Chauncy's hirsutely cespitose ears in the least attractive.*

twisted, *adj.* tortuous; tortile: *Capicola used his tortile reasoning to convince Eselkopf to buy his old car.*

twofold, *adj.* diploid: *My ratiocination for declination is diploid—I haven't the time, and I haven't the money.*

two-sided, *adj.* dihedral; bilateral: *That's a dihedral question.*

U

unavoidable, *adj.* see **inescapable.**

uncouth, *adj.* agrestic: *Lem's agrestic behaviour would make him an unwelcome guest in anyone's home.*

undeniable, *adj.* irrefragable: *Twerply's contention that his intelligence was unequalled anywhere is an irrefragable fact.*

underground, *adj.* hypogene: *Camparsita started a hypogene newspaper when she was a student at the Sorbonne.*

unforgivable, *adj.* see **unpardonable.**

unifying, *adj.* esemplastic: *Membership in the Paphian group has had an esemplastic effect on us all.*

unique, *adj.* (unique quality) haecceity: *Dumbauer has a certain haecceity that makes him a valuable employee in our toilet tissue recycling plant.*

unisex, *adj.* diclinous: *There is a diclinous hairdresser in the High street.* epicene; gynandromorph: *There is no garment more epicene than blue jeans.*

unkempt, *adj.* raggle-taggle; raddled: *I say, Old Bean, you look a bit raddled. Did you fall into your gin and it?*

unpardonable, *adj.* inexpiable: *Bringing along your pet mongoose to play with Lady Ginbibber's pet boa constrictor was an inexpiable faux pas.*

unsophisticated, *adj.* see naive.

unthinkable, *adj.* incogitable: *Accepting another invitation from the Rasmussens for a dinner of raw tripe salad would be incogitable.*

uproot, *vb.* deracinate; extirpate: *Thousands were deracinated during the war.*

urban, *adj.* oppidan: *I'd gladly support the oppidan revitalization programme if I knew what it was.*

urinating, *adj.* micturant; (backwards) retromingent: *You retromingent, dicephalic, dysthymic oaf! Get out of my way!*

V

vagrant, *n.* see **beggar.**

varied, *adj.* multifarious: *Among his multifarious talents Mustapha Ogosh includes rolling a six-inch hoop.*

veal, *n.* vituline: *I hope, Mrs. Grimp, that you will be able to join us for a vituline repast this evening?*

W

wander, *vb.* divagate: *They found father at the other side of town, divagating among the demimondes.*

warehouse, *n.* see **storehouse.**

warming, *adj.* calefacient, calefactory: *On cold nights, I would get into Martha's bed, and her calefactory body soon made me quite comfortable.*

warty, *adj.* verrucous, verrucose: *Rumour has it that Oxonia's verrucose complexion unduly influenced the judges in the Miss Universe contest.*

wash, *vb.* perform (one's) ablutions: *Please perform your ablutions before coming in for dinner.*

washing, *n.* lavation: *I expect you, Fingal, to engage in manual lavation prior to prandial activity.*

waste, *n.* egesta. (excrete waste) egest. (excretion of waste) egestion: *I excused myself for a moment, explaining that I had a matter of egestion to attend to.*

watery, *adj.* irriguous: *Clementine looked deep into Dorpfinger's irriguous eyes and became almost seasick.*

waver, *vb.* librate: *I am librating between going to a seafood restaurant and eating a salami sandwich at home.*

weak, *adj.* asthenic: *Philibeg is far too asthenic to attempt a single-handed crossing of the river, let alone the Atlantic.*

weakening, *n.* labefaction: *Deirdre Wagstaff's refusal to speak to me is indicative of the labefaction of our relationship.*

weak-minded, *adj.* cachectic: *Lord Ballotine is getting a bit cachectic in his advancing years.*

weariness, *n.* lassitude: *After filling us with good wine, our host overwhelmed us with lassitude as he described, in interminable detail, how he'd bought it.*

weekly, *adj.* hebdomadary, hebdomadal: *From the mephitic fetor in this place, I'd suggest you break your schedule of a hebdomadal bath and have one immediately.*

western, *adj.* occidental: *The gunfighters faced each other in an occidental encounter.*

whisper, *vb.* susurrate: *Quasimodo doesn't like the girls to susurrate behind his back.*

whitening, *adj.* albescent: *Featherstonehaugh's hair is albescent at the temples.*

winged, *adj.* alate: *'. . . Time's alate chariot drawing near.'*

wink, *vb.* palpebrate: *I palpebrated at her slyly across the room.*

wintry, *adj.* brumal: *When she caught me leering at Prunella, my wife gave me a brumal look.*

wish, *n.* velleity: *If velleities were equines, tatterdemalions would equitate.*

woman-hater, *n.* misogynist: *I cannot imagine why you think that Ponce de León was a misogynist.*

wooded, *adj.* (thickly wooded) arboreous: *Heathcliff led Rosanna into an arboreous copse, where they continued their conversation.*

wooden-headed, *adj.* xylocephalic: *Henry Schmerz is so xylocephalic that when I told him so, he took it as a compliment.*

woolly, *adj.* lanate, lanose: *Sigrid wore her coif like a lanose halo.*

work of art, *n.* oeuvre: *When Oskar Fester became chef in charge of hors d'oeuvres, his chef-d'oeuvre was oeufs à la Russe.*

wooded, *adj.* (thickly wooded) arboreous:
*Heathcliff led Rosanna into an arboreous
copse, where they continued their conversation.*

worldly, *adj.* mundane; terrene: *When Lucy and Cecil Rowbotham broke up, she took away all his terrene possessions, including his soup tureen and his terrine de veau.*

wormlike, *adj.* lumbricoid: *Snively pulled one of his lumbricoid tricks again when he threatened to tell Lord Haildon that his wife was fooling around.*

worn-out, *adj.* see **decrepit.**

would-be, *adj.* manqué: *Crumford isn't exactly a fool, he's more of a genius manqué.*

wrinkled, *adj.* rugose: *Prunella Dermato's rugose face looked like an aerial view of the Nile delta.*

Y

yard, *n.* see **garden.**

Index

antiphon ANSWER
antipodal OPPOSITE
antipodean OPPOSITE
apian BEELIKE
apodictic TRUE
apopemptic GOODBYE
apotheosis IDEAL
appanage PERQUISITE
appetence DESIRE
appetency DESIRE
aquiline EAGLELIKE
arachnoid SPIDERY
arboreous WOODED
arcana MYSTERY
arcuate BENT
arenose SANDY
armillary BRACELET
aroint thee SCRAM
arras TAPESTRY
arrivisme AMBITION
arundinaceous REEDLIKE
ascesis SELF-DISCIPLINE
asthenic WEAK
asymptotic APPROACHING
ataractic CALMING
atrabilious IRRITABLE
aureate ORNATE
austral SOUTHERN
australopithecine APELIKE
autecious PARASITIC
autochthonous NATIVE
avatar MANIFESTATION
avian BIRDLIKE
avuncular FRIENDLY
bacilliform ROD-SHAPED
baculiform ROD-SHAPED

bagatelle TRIFLE
baksheesh TIP
balneal BATHING
banausic MECHANICAL
barbellate BRISTLY
bathetic TRITE
bayadère STRIPED
beldam HAG
bêtise FOLLY
bicuspidate POINTED
bifurcate FORKED
bifurcation FORKED
bilabial click KISS
bilateral TWO-SIDED
borborygmal RUMBLING
borborygmic RUMBLING
borborygmus RUMBLING
boreal NORTHERN
botryoidal GRAPELIKE
botryose GRAPELIKE
bovine COWLIKE
boyla DOCTOR
brachylogous CONCISE
bradyencephalic SLOW
bradyencephalous SLOW
bromhidrosis SWEAT
bromide BORE
brontoid THUNDEROUS
brumal WINTRY
bubaline BUFFALOLIKE
buccal ORAL
bulimia HUNGER
bursiform POUCH-SHAPED
cabbalistic SECRET
cachectic WEAK-MINDED
cachinnate LAUGH

cachinnation LAUGH
cacoepistic MISPRONUNCIATION
cacoepy MISPRONUNCIATION
cacoethes MANIA
cacography MISSPELLING
caducity PERISHABLENESS, SENILITY
cafard DEPRESSION
calefacient WARMING
calefactory WARMING
caprine LUSTFUL
cespitose TUFTED
Cicerone GUIDE
crepitate CRACKLE
decollate SEPARATE
decollation SEPARATE
decorticate PEEL
decrement DECREASE
decumbent PRONE
decussate INTERSECT
defalcate EMBEZZLE
defalcation EMBEZZLE
dégagé CASUAL, RELAXED
deglutition SWALLOWING
deipnosophist CONVERSATIONALIST
deipnosophy CONVERSATIONALIST
deliquesce ABSORB
deliquescent ABSORB
Delphic OBSCURE
démarche MANOEUVRE
demotic POPULAR
deontic OBLIGATORY
depilate SHAVE

depurate CLEANSE, PURIFY
deracinate UPROOT
descant COMMENT
despumate PURIFY
desquamate PEEL
desuetude DISUSE
detumesce SOFTEN
detumescence SOFTEN
devitrify OPAQUE
devoirs COURTESIES
dexter FAVOURABLE
dextrorse SPIRAL
dharma DUTY
diablerie MISCHIEF
diastasis SEPARATE
diastema GAP
diathesis SUSCEPTIBLE
diathetic SUSCEPTIBLE
dichotomize DIVIDE, SPLIT
dichotomy DIVIDE
diclinous UNISEX
dicynodont BUCK-TOOTHED
digitigrade TIPTOE
dihedral TWO-SIDED
diluvial FLOOD
diluvium FLOOD
dimidiate HALVE
diploid TWOFOLD
disaffirm DENY
disaffirmation DENY
discommode DISTURB, INCONVENIENCE
disembogue FLOW
disject SCATTER
disjecta membra FRAGMENTS, SCATTER

disoblige SLIGHT
disprize DISDAIN
distrait ABSENT-MINDED
distraite ABSENT-MINDED
dithyrambic ELOQUENT
divagate DIGRESS, WANDER
doit TRIFLE
dolabriform HATCHET-SHAPED
dotage SENILITY
douceur TIP
dragoman GUIDE
dragonnade PERSECUTE
dragoon FORCE
dulosis SLAVERY
dyslogistic DISAPPROVING
dysphoric ILL-AT-EASE
ebullition OUTBURST
ecaudate TAILLESS
ecchymosed BLACK-AND-BLUE
ecchymosis BLACK-AND-BLUE
ecchymotic BLACK-AND-BLUE
echinate BRISTLY
echt GENUINE
ectype COPY
edacious GREEDY
edacity GREEDY
edentate TOOTHLESS
edentulous TOOTHLESS
edulcorate CLEANSE
effloresce BLOOM
effluvium STENCH
effulgent RADIANT
egest WASTE
egesta WASTE
egestion WASTE

egregious BAD
eleemosynary CHARITABLE
embonpoint STOUTNESS
embrocation LOTION
emolument SALARY
empyreuma BURNING
encaenia DEDICATION
encephalic BRAIN
encephalon BRAIN
enchorial NATIVE
energumen FANATIC
epicene EFFEMINATE, UNISEX
epigone IMITATOR
epistaxis NOSEBLEED
epistle LETTER
equiponderate OFFSET
erethismic EXCITABLE
erethistic EXCITABLE
erethitic EXCITABLE
eristic ARGUMENTATIVE
eruct BELCH
eructate BELCH
eructation BELCH
esemplastic UNIFYING
esurient GREEDY
euchre CHEAT
eudemonia HAPPINESS
eudemonic HAPPINESS
evaginate INSIDE OUT
excaudate TAILLESS
exiguous MEAGRE
exsert PROTRUDE
extirpate UPROOT
exuviate SHED
fer-de-lance SNAKE
florid ORNATE
furcate FORKED

furcation FORKED
galère CLAQUE
galimatias GIBBERISH
galliard GAY
gallinaceous HENLIKE
gambado CAPER
gangrel BEGGAR
gangue RUBBISH
garth GARDEN
gasconade BRAGGING
gavage STUFF
Gemeinschaft COMMUNITY
glabrous BALD
glaucous BLUISH-GREEN
glomerular CLUSTER
glomerulus CLUSTER
gluteal BUTTOCKS
gnathonic FLATTERING,
 TOADYING
goatish LUSTFUL
godown STOREHOUSE
goliard STUDENT
Gongorism OBSCURE
gongoristic INTRICATE
gormless DULL
gossoon SERVANT
gowk PERSON
grallatorial LONG-LEGGED
gramineous GRASSLIKE
graminivorous GRASS-
 EATING
grumous GRANULAR
gudgeon BAIT, ENTICEMENT
guerdon REWARD
guidon FLAG
gulosity GLUTTONY
gurry OFFAL

gynandromorph UNISEX
haecceity UNIQUE
harridan NAG
haruspicy DIVINATION
hebdomadal WEEKLY
hebdomadary WEEKLY
hebetude LETHARGY
hebetudinous THICK-
 HEADED
helminth PARASITIC
helminthic PARASITIC
helotism SLAVERY
hepatic DISAGREEABLE
hermeneutic INTERPRETIVE
hierophant INTERPRETER
hircine LUSTFUL
hispid HAIRY
horal HOURLY
horatory ENCOURAGING
hortative ENCOURAGING
hyaline TRANSPARENT
hyetal RAINY
hypogene UNDERGROUND
iatric MEDICAL
ichthyic FISHY
ichthyoid FISHLIKE
ignescent FLAMMABLE
imbricate OVERLAPPING
inchoation BEGINNING
incogitable UNTHINKABLE
incogitant THOUGHTLESS
incondite CRUDE
incrassate SWOLLEN
incunabula BEGINNINGS
indigent POVERTY-STRICKEN
indurate CALLOUS
ineluctable INESCAPABLE

inexpiable UNPARDONABLE
infundibular FUNNEL-
   SHAPED
infundibuliform FUNNEL-
   SHAPED
infuscate BROWN
ingeminate REPEAT
innocuous HARMLESS
inosculate BLEND
intenerate TENDERIZE
involution COMPLICATION
iracund IRRITABLE
irrefragable UNDENIABLE
irriguous WATERY
jactitation BOASTING
jejune DULL, NAIVE
jeremiad LAMENT
keratoid HORNY
labefaction WEAKENING
lachrymose SAD
lacuna GAP
lacustrine LAKESHORE
lambent BRIGHT, RADIANT
lanate WOOLLY
lancinate CUTTING
lanose WOOLLY
laodicean INDIFFERENT
lassitude WEARINESS
lavation WASHING
lecherous LUSTFUL
lenitive SOOTHING
levigate SMOOTH
librate WAVER
littoral SEASHORE
logorrhea TALKATIVE
logorrheic TALKATIVE

longanimity PATIENCE
longueur BOREDOM
louche SHIFTY
lubricious LEWDNESS
lubricity LEWDNESS
lubricous LEWDNESS
luculent CLEAR
lugubrious MOURNFUL
lumbricoid WORMLIKE
lyncean SHARP-EYED
macedoine MIXTURE
macrencephalia BIG-
   BRAINED
macrencephalic BIG-
   BRAINED
macrencephaly BIG-
   BRAINED
macula FRECKLED
macular FRECKLED
maculate POLLUTE
maculation POLLUTE
maenad SHREW
malapert IMPUDENT
malversation MISCONDUCT
manducate CHEW
manqué WOULD-BE
mansuetude GENTLE
mansuetudinous GENTLE
marabunta SHREW
masticate CHEW
mattoid INSANE
melanoid DARK-COLOURED
melanous BRUNET(TE)
mendacious LIE
mendacity LIE
menthaceous MINTY

mephitic HARMFUL, PUTRID
meretricious INSINCERE
microcephalic PIN-HEADED
micturant URINATING
minacious THREATENING
minatorial THREATENING
minatory THREATENING
minify BELITTLE
misanthrope MAN-HATER
misogynist WOMAN-HATER
missive LETTER
moiety HALF
molluscoid CLAMMY
mordacious SARCASTIC
mucid MOULDY, SLIMY
mucronate POINTED
muliebrity FEMININITY
multifarious VARIED
mundane WORLDLY
munificence GENEROSITY
myrmidon HENCHMAN
nadir DEPTHS
nanocerebral DIMWITTED
narcoleptic SLEEPY
natant FLOATING
natatorium SWIMMING
  POOL
necessitous POVERTY-
  STRICKEN
neoteric NEW
nescience IGNORANT
nescient IGNORANT
nexus LINK
nictitate BLINK
nimiety EXCESS,
  OVERABUNDANCE

ninnyhammer FOOL
nitid BRIGHT
niveous SNOWY
nocent HARMFUL
nociceptive PAINFUL
nocuous HARMFUL
nodus PROBLEM
noxious HARMFUL
nugatory TRIFLING
nullifidian SCEPTIC
numen PRINCIPLE
numina PRINCIPLE
numinous MYSTERIOUS
nutational NODDING
obfuscate BEWILDER
obfuscatory BEWILDER
objurgate SCOLD
obmutescent SILENT
obnubilate OBSCURE
obsecrate IMPLORE
obtest IMPLORE
obvolution ROLL
occidental WESTERN
oeillade OGLE
oeuvre WORK OF ART
on the qui vive ALERT
operose BUSY
oppidan URBAN
oppugn DISPUTE
oppugnant CONTRARY,
  DISPUTE
orgulous PROUD
oriental EASTERN
orotund POMPOUS
oscitance LAZY
oscitancy LAZY

oscitant LAZY
oscitantion LAZY
osmidrosis SWEAT
otiose LAZY
ovine SHEEPLIKE
padang PLAYING-FIELD
pagurian RECLUSIVE
paillasse MATTRESS
pakeha NONNATIVE
palliasse MATTRESS
palmary PRAISEWORTHY
palpebrate BLINK, WINK
paludal MARSHY
pandect TREATISE
panga KNIFE
panicle TUFT
panmixia MATE
panmixis MATE
papaveraceous POPPYLIKE
papilionaceous
    BUTTERFLYLIKE
parachronism LATENESS
paraclete MEDIATOR
paradigm MODEL
paragon MODEL
parang KNIFE
paranymph BEST MAN,
    BRIDESMAID
pasquinade RIDICULE
patellate PAN-SHAPED
patriclinous FATHERLIKE
patulous OPEN-MOUTHED,
    SPREADING
pavid AFRAID, FEARFUL
pavonine PEACOCKLIKE
pedicular LOUSY
penetralia SECRETS

perform ablutions WASH
prochronism EARLINESS
quaggy FLABBY
quaquaversal RADIATING
quaternity FOURSOME
quelquechose TRIFLE
quidnunc GOSSIPMONGER
quondam FORMER
raddled UNKEMPT
raggle-taggle UNKEMPT
rallentando SLOWING
rammish LUSTFUL
randy LUSTFUL
rasorial SCRAPING
rath EAGER
rathe EAGER
rebarbative FORBIDDING
réchauffé CHESTNUT
recherché CHOICE
réclame PUBLICITY
recreant COWARDLY
recrement REFUSE
recrudesce RECUR
recusant REBEL
renitent INFLEXIBLE
reptant CRAWLING
res gestae ACHIEVEMENTS
resipiscence CONFESSION
retromingent URINATING
rictal OPEN-MOUTHED
rident LAUGHING
ritardando SLOWING
ritenuto SLOWING
roborant STRENGTHENING
rubescence BLUSHING
rubescent BLUSHING
rugose WRINKLED

ruttish LUSTFUL
sabulose SANDY
sabulosity SANDY
sabulous SANDY
sakai BOOR
salubrious HEALTHY
saponaceous SOAPY
scabrous INDECENT
scrobiculate PITTED
scrofulous DEGRADED
sequacious PLIANT
sesquipedalian
    MULTISYLLABIC
setaceous BRISTLY
shandrydan JALOPY
shrew NAG
simulacra SEMBLANCE
simulacrum SEMBLANCE
singultus HICCUP
sinistrorse SPIRAL
sortilege MAGIC
sough SIGH
spavined DECRIPIT
sternutate SNEEZE
sthenic ACTIVE
struthious OSTRICHLIKE
subereous CORKY
suberic CORKY
suberose CORKY
sulphurous HOT-TEMPERED
sumptuary EXTRAVAGANT
supernatant FLOATING
suspire SIGH
susurrate WHISPER
sycophantic TOADYING
synchronic CONTEMPORARY

tachyencephalic QUICK
tachyencephalous QUICK
tantivy RAPIDLY
taurine OPTIMISTIC
tenebrous SHADOWY
tergiversate EQUIVOCATE
termagant NAG, SHREW
terrene WORLDLY
tetrachromatic FOUR-
    COLOUR
tetrachrome FOUR-COLOUR
thetic ARBITRARY
thrasonical BOASTFUL
tortile TWISTED
tortuous TWISTED
tracasserie ANNOYANCE
tumescent BULGING
tumid BULGING
umbrageous SHADY
ungular HOOFLIKE
ursine PESSIMISTIC
velleity WISH
venery HUNTING
verecund SHY
verjuice SOUR
verjuiced SOUR
verrucose WARTY
verrucous WARTY
vilipend SLANDER
villatic RUSTIC
vituline VEAL
walla SUPERVISOR
wallah SUPERVISOR
xylocephalic WOODEN-
    HEADED
zealot FANATIC

CLAURÈNE DUGRAN studied linguistics at Oxford and drama at Cambridge. *Wordsmanship* represents her lifelong ambition to combine both fields by creating more dramatic dictionaries. The example sentences, drawn from real life, are populated by people she has known through the years.

Mme duGran is married and lives with her husband in Mysborne, Kent, where they raise flies for trout fishermen.